A Book to Help Children and Families

Up and Down the Worry Hill

A Children's Book about Obsessive-Compulsive Disorder and its Treatment

By Aureen Pinto Wagner, Ph.D.

Illustrations by Paul A. Jutton

A Lighthouse Press Book

FIND YOUR BEARINGS, REACH YOUR GOALS

Publisher's Cataloging-in-Publication
(Provided by Quality Books, Inc.)

Wagner, Aureen Pinto.
    Up and down the worry hill : a children's book
about obsessive-compulsive disorder and its
treatment / by Aureen Pinto Wagner ; illustrations
by Paul A. Jutton. -- 1st ed.
    p. cm.
    SUMMARY: An examination of compulsive behavior,
focusing on the fact that those who suffer from
this disorder are not alone nor are to blame for
having it. The causes, effects, and treatment of
the illness are also discussed.

    1. Obsessive-compulsive disorder in children--
Juvenile literature.   I. Jutton, Paul A.
II. Title.

RJ506.O252000   618.92'85227
                             QBI99-500578

Library of Congress Catalog Card Number 99-97628

Copyright, ©2000

by Aureen Pinto Wagner, Ph.D.

Published by Lighthouse Press, Inc.,

Toll free USA 1-888-749-8768

www.Lighthouse-Press.com

ISBN 0-9677347-0-3

Printed in the United States of America

to all the courageous children who have taught me about

the struggles and victories of being a child with OCD.

With thanks to my husband, Scott, who first inspired me to write this book,

and with whose continued support this book was made possible,

to our children Catherine and Ethan, and to my parents and family

for their love and confidence in me through the years.

Preface for Parents and Professionals

In the course of my experience as a Clinical Child Psychologist, parents have often asked me to recommend books on Obsessive-Compulsive Disorder (OCD) that their children could read and understand. Having had this question raised repeatedly, I decided to respond to this important need by writing **Up and Down the Worry Hill**.

When children experience obsessions and compulsions, they are often scared, confused, ashamed and defensive, as they cannot explain why they feel compelled to behave in certain ways. This book is written to address the needs and questions of these children. Children need to know that they are not the only ones with OCD and that neither they nor their parents are to blame for it. They need to know that help is available and that they can have a significant impact on their own treatment and recovery.

Up and Down the Worry Hill describes OCD from a child's perspective. It attempts to give children with OCD a sense of control and hope in their lives. Hope and optimism are major factors in building the motivation and persistence that it takes to gain mastery over OCD.

This book is designed for parents or professionals and children to read together. It offers parents, educators and clinicians the chance to engage in an open discussion of a difficult topic, and to provide accurate information about OCD. It is intended to help children dispel fears and uncertainties and prepare to engage in treatment.

In particular, **Up and Down the Worry Hill** focuses on describing Behavior Therapy for OCD in a manner that children can comprehend.

This book uses real-life metaphors to describe OCD and its treatment. Metaphors simplify difficult and abstract concepts by comparing them to situations that children can easily understand. The metaphors I have used in this book evolved over the years in my work with children with OCD. The children I have treated have responded very favorably to the metaphor of the "Worry Hill".

To make the best use of this book, read and discuss this story repeatedly with your child. Repeated readings will help your child absorb and integrate the many complexities of OCD gradually. Young children may benefit from having segments of the book read to them at different times.

This book was not designed to replace professional consultation and treatment, which is strongly recommended for children with OCD.

Parents and professionals are encouraged to read the companion book, **WHAT TO DO WHEN YOUR CHILD HAS OBSESSIVE-COMPULSIVE DISORDER: STRATEGIES AND SOLUTIONS** for a discussion of diagnosis, treatment options, parenting tips and strategies, school issues, and answers to questions.

Aureen P. Wagner, Ph.D.

Casey woke up and rubbed his eyes. It was a bright and sunny day.

He was happy and wanted to ride the new bicycle his parents gave him.
He had been practicing everyday and could ride it pretty well.

Daddy had said that once Casey could ride a bicycle well, he would teach him how to ride
up the Big Hill at the end of the street and then coast down it.
Casey had been waiting to do that for a long time. Today was the day...

Casey sat up in bed.
He picked up Teddy and touched him four times.
Then he got out of bed carefully, with one foot first, then the other.

He patted his pillow four times and tucked his sheets all around it.

Casey smiled. "It just feels right. Now I'll have a perfect day."

"Mommy, I'm up! I want to go out and ride my new bike."

"Come on down, Casey," replied his mother. "Daddy and Jenny are up too.
It's time for breakfast, and then off to school you go. You can ride your bike when you
get home from school in the afternoon."

Casey started to get dressed for school. He put on his "special" pants.
They felt right. His other pants always felt like they were going to fall down.
Then he picked out the "special" socks that stayed up just under his knees.
He had many other pairs of socks, but none of them stayed up as well.
He opened and shut his bedroom door a few times.

He counted the stairs as he went down. "That wasn't right," he said.
   He went back up and counted them again...
      And again...

"I wish I could get it right the first time,"
Casey sighed.

"Look, Casey, I made muffins for you,"
said his mother, giving him a big hug and a kiss.

"Oh, goody! My favorite kind," grinned
Casey. "But my hands feel dirty.
I have to wash them."

Casey scrubbed his hands
well and rinsed them.
Then he looked
at them carefully.
"They still feel yucky.
What if there are any
germs on them?"
He washed his hands again.

Casey's mother came in. "Are you done
washing, dear?" Casey was getting
frustrated. "My hands feel germy.
I have to wash them again."

Casey's mother looked at his hands.
"They're very clean. Now turn off the
faucet, or you'll be late for school," she said.

Casey looked at his mother. "Would you please turn off the faucet for me? I can't do it
myself." Casey's mother turned off the faucet and helped him out of the bathroom.

Casey sat down for breakfast after giving his Dad a hug.
His sister Jenny ate her muffins and drank her juice fast.
His parents sipped their coffee and talked
about the new bicycles they got
for Casey and Jenny.

But Casey wasn't listening. He was busy cutting his muffin up into small pieces, all the same size. He ate one piece on one side of his mouth, then took one sip of his juice, and ate the next piece on the other side of his mouth.

Then he repeated it all over again.

Casey's mother looked at the clock. "It's time for the school bus, Casey! Just take a few bites all at once and you'll be done before you know it."

Casey looked at his plate. He had seven bites left and he had to finish them in the right order.

"I can't eat any faster, I have to do it exactly this way," he whispered to himself.

Jenny laughed at him. "C'mon Casey-man, what's the matter? Can't you hurry, slow-poke? I saw you this morning, touching and counting things in your room. You're weird, Casey!"

Casey was sad. He finished his muffin just in time for the school bus.

Then he had to check his book bag
to make sure he hadn't forgotten anything.
He counted his books, pencils, and erasers.

Jenny started talking just then,
and Casey thought he made a mistake.
He counted everything again,
just to be sure.

As he rushed out for the bus,
he wondered if he counted it right.

At school, the teacher, Mrs. Kelly, said it was going to be a fun day.
"We're going to learn about the sun, the moon, and the planets today.
Then you can draw and paint them!"

Casey was excited. He knew the names of all the planets and he couldn't wait to say them. Then suddenly, he felt scared. He thought about drawing and painting the planets. What if the paint got on his hands and he couldn't wash it off? Would it make him sick?

He asked Mrs. Kelly if he would get sick. "No, Casey, you'll be fine," she said.

But Casey couldn't stop thinking about it. He asked Mrs. Kelly again.
She told him again that he would be fine.

Casey began to draw all the planets. He wanted his drawing to be perfect.
The circles didn't come out right, so he erased them and drew them again.
His drawing still wasn't perfect. Casey erased it again. The paper tore.

Casey was getting tired.
The other kids had finished their drawings and were painting them.

Everyone was having so much fun. Why couldn't he be like them?
He felt ashamed and hid his drawing.

Pete and Laura were sitting next to Casey.
Pete said, "Hey, how come you're always the last
one to finish anything, Casey?" Laura ran over and
said, "Let me see your drawing! The paper's torn.
How come you have to erase everything?"

Casey looked away. He didn't know what to say.
He wished he could hide somewhere or disappear.
He couldn't wait to get home.

Mrs. Kelly came over to Casey's desk and asked if
he needed help. Casey shook his head and said,
"I'm fine, thank you."

Finally, it was time for Casey to go home.
He was tired but excited.

At last, his Dad was home from work. It was time to ride up the Big Hill! Casey and his father put on their helmets and off they went.

Daddy said, "Remember, Casey, it's hard work to get to the top of the hill. You have to keep going a little at a time. I'll be right with you if you need any help."

"I really want to do it, Daddy! I know I can!"

As they went up the hill, Casey began huffing and puffing. He kept saying, "I can do it, little by little."

And then...

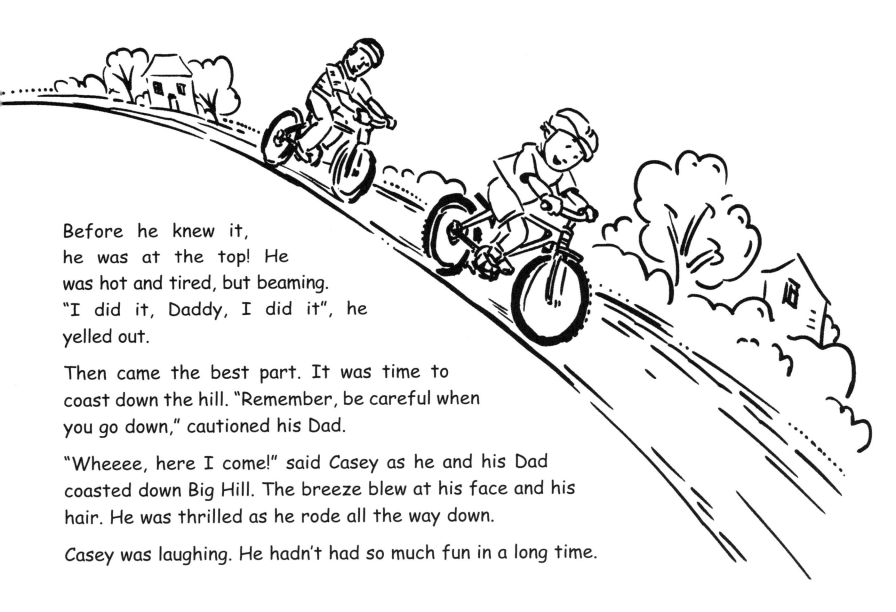

Before he knew it,
he was at the top! He
was hot and tired, but beaming.
"I did it, Daddy, I did it", he
yelled out.

Then came the best part. It was time to
coast down the hill. "Remember, be careful when
you go down," cautioned his Dad.

"Wheeee, here I come!" said Casey as he and his Dad
coasted down Big Hill. The breeze blew at his face and his
hair. He was thrilled as he rode all the way down.

Casey was laughing. He hadn't had so much fun in a long time.

Casey and his Dad rested at the bottom of Big Hill. Casey's Dad said, "You're a great kid, Casey."

"But Daddy, I don't get things right the first time. I have to do things over and over again."

"Mommy and I love you the same, no matter what," replied his father, patting him on the back.

That night, Casey's mother came to tuck him into bed. She sat at his bedside. "You look tired and sad, Casey. Is everything ok? I saw you pulling up your pajamas again and again like they wouldn't stay up. Mrs. Kelly said you were trying very hard to get your drawing right at school."

Casey's eyes filled with tears. "Mommy, I try so hard to do things perfectly but it's so hard. Something tells me I have to do it right or something bad will happen. Why do I have to do that? How come Jenny doesn't need to do that?"

Casey's mother kissed him on the forehead. "Nobody's perfect, Casey. Each kid is different in his or her own way," she replied. "But that doesn't mean that you are not good or smart.

And we love you no matter what. Let's go talk to Dr. Greene tomorrow to see how she can help you."

Casey felt a lot better after that. He smiled and went to sleep.

Dr. Greene was a special doctor called a child psychologist. Casey was nervous about talking to her, but she was kind and gentle. She listened quietly as Casey and his parents told her that he had to do a lot of things over and over again.

"Do you like having to repeat things over, Casey?" asked Dr. Greene. "No, I wish I could stop because I'd like to play and have fun like the other kids."

"What happens if you try not to do it again, Casey?" asked Dr. Greene. "I feel funny, kind of scared and kind of weird. Sometimes it makes me upset. Something tells me I have to do it to feel good. Sometimes I don't know why I do it, but I just have to."

"Is there something wrong with me, Dr. Greene? Am I the only one who has to do things this way?"

"No, Casey, you're just like any other kid except that you have an illness called **Obsessive-Compulsive Disorder**. It's called **OCD** for short. Let me tell you a little bit about OCD.

You see, Casey, OCD is something that happens in your brain. Your brain is like a computer. It does many things and is very busy. When you have OCD, your brain's computer tells you to worry about things that are not true and tells you to do things over again even when you don't need to. It happens because some chemicals in your brain don't work right, and your brain gets "stuck".

It's like it would be if you rang the doorbell and the button got stuck. The doorbell would keep ringing and ringing loudly and wouldn't know when to stop. OCD is like a "worry button" in your brain that gets stuck and doesn't stop.

The worry thoughts that OCD puts in your brain are called **obsessions**. The things you do over and over again to make the worry thoughts go away are called **compulsions** or **rituals**."

Casey was surprised to hear that he had something called OCD that happened in his brain. "So it's not just my fault that I do weird things, is it Dr. Greene?" he asked. Dr. Greene replied, "Not at all! Having OCD is not your fault. It's not your parents' fault either. It's like having allergies or asthma—it happens to you because you're more sensitive to it. Sometimes there are other people in your family who are also sensitive to it and have OCD.

OCD doesn't happen because you've been bad or because you do it on purpose. Sometimes, your parents or your teachers and friends may think that you are just being stubborn or annoying. It's hard for them to understand that you don't want to do it, but you can't stop." Casey's parents nodded their heads.

"Will I always have to do things over and over, Dr. Greene?"

Dr. Greene smiled at Casey and his parents and said, "I have some good news for you. There are some ways to fix your "worry button" when it gets stuck. One way is to learn how to tell OCD to stop bothering you by learning some special exercises. This way is called **Behavior Therapy**.

In Behavior Therapy you learn some exercises that teach you how to face your OCD worries and find out that they are not true. Then you learn to stop doing the things OCD tells you to do. It's a lot like riding a bicycle. Do you ride a bicycle, Casey?"

"Yes, yes, I just rode up a big hill yesterday and then I came coasting down. It was hard work to get up the hill, but lots of fun coming down," said Casey with sparkling eyes.

"Well, Casey, learning how to stop OCD is a lot like that. In the beginning, stopping your rituals feels like riding up a big "Worry Hill" because it gets harder. If you keep going and don't give up, you get to the top of the "Worry Hill". Once you get to the top, it's easy to come down the hill. You can only coast down the hill if you first get to the top.

Getting to the top of the "Worry Hill" takes patience and hard work. Repeating to yourself, "I want to," makes it a lot easier. The more you practice, the easier it gets.

The exercises you will learn are called **exposure and ritual prevention**. I will help you learn how to do these exercises. You will learn that nothing bad will happen if you stop doing the things OCD wants you to do.

Your parents will encourage you and cheer you on, but you're the one who has to learn how to ride up the hill, and you're the one who has to face OCD and tell it to go away."

"Another way to make OCD better is to take **medicine**. The medicine makes the chemicals in your brain work properly again. It takes a few weeks to make the OCD better, and sometimes, it takes a while to find the right medicine.

Not every kid needs medicine. Some kids need both medicine and Behavior Therapy to get better. Medicine can sometimes make it easier to learn the exposure and ritual prevention exercises. Dr. Murphy, who is a child psychiatrist, knows all about the best medicines for OCD, and can help you understand all about it if you need medicine."

Casey and his parents were happy to hear about Behavior Therapy and the medicine that could help him with his OCD.

"Casey, did you know that there are many other kids and adults who also have OCD? You're not the only one!

Everyone's OCD can be a little different—sometimes kids have obsessions about someone getting hurt or bad luck happening or even bad thoughts.

Rituals can be of different types, like checking things, or counting or cleaning and tidying.

I can help you meet other kids and families who also have OCD, so you can see that you are not alone and that other kids get better too."

Casey felt happy and relieved. Suddenly, he didn't feel crazy, scared, or confused any more.

"Yes!" he said. "I want to learn the exercises to make the OCD go away."

Casey's parents hugged him. "Dad and I will do everything to help you learn how to beat OCD," said his mother.

Casey began to see Dr. Greene every week after school. He learned the exposure and ritual prevention exercises.

Little by little, Casey learned how to walk down the stairs without stopping and counting, wash his hands only once before eating, take big bites of his muffin and go to the bus stop without checking his book bag.

Dr. Greene was right! At first, he felt worried and scared when he didn't do the rituals, but pretty soon, he found that the scared feeling just went away!

Casey practiced the new things he learned everyday. The more he practiced, the less worried he felt, and the easier it became. His "worry button" didn't seem to get stuck as much anymore.

Dr. Greene also talked to Casey's parents to teach them ways to help Casey face his OCD, and to be patient and understanding.

Casey also met Tim, Stacy, Laurie, Kevin, and Nancy at the OCD Kids Group, who were a lot like him. They all talked about their OCD. Sometimes they laughed at the silly things OCD made them do. Soon they became friends.

Casey knew he was not alone. He knew he was normal, just like any other kid.

Casey started feeling a lot better. After a few weeks, he noticed that he didn't worry as much or feel sad anymore. He didn't have to touch things four times any more. He could eat his muffins just as fast as Jenny! His clothes didn't feel so funny and slippery now. His hands didn't feel so "germy" anymore. He even forgot to check his book bag before he ran off to school!

Most of all, he found out that he didn't have to be perfect! He was having fun like the other kids.

Then one day, Casey
rode his bicycle up the Big
Hill all by himself! He wasn't huffing
and puffing as much anymore. He got to
the top quickly and looked around. He was so
proud of himself. Then it was time for his
favorite part—coasting down the Big Hill. As he
breezed past the bushes and trees, he whistled a tune
and thought to himself, "I learned how to ride up the hill
and I learned how to face my OCD. I wish I could tell other
kids with OCD who feel alone, ashamed, and sad, Don't give up! You
too can learn how to ride up and down the Worry Hill and beat OCD."

Casey began singing to himself, "Up the hill, down the hill, on my
new bicycle..."

Lighthouse Press: ORDER FORM

NAME: _____

ADDRESS: _____

CITY: _____ STATE: _____ ZIP: _____ COUNTRY: _____

TELEPHONE: _____ E-MAIL ADDRESS: _____

Please send me _____ copies of *Up and Down the Worry Hill* by Aureen P. Wagner, Ph.D. for **$16.95** per book.

Quantity discount: If you are ordering at least 5 copies, deduct 15% from the total cost of the books.
Sales Tax: Please add applicable sales tax for those orders shipped to addresses in New York State.

SHIPPING AND HANDLING:

US: Add $3 shipping and handling for the first book and $1 for each additional book. **Canada:** Add $6 shipping and handling for the first book and $2 for each additional book. **Other International:** Please add $9 for the first book and $5 for each additional book.

ORDER TOTAL	
$16.95 Per book x _____ books . . . . $_____	
Quantity Discount (Subtract 15% if ordering 5 or more copies) – $_____	
New York State Sales Tax . . . . $_____	
Shipping and Handling (US/Canada/Int'l) . . . . $_____	
TOTAL . . . . $_____	

All orders must be prepaid by check/money order in US funds (checks drawn on US banks). Check enclosed for the amount of: $ _____

I am a/an:

☐ Parent   ☐ Psychologist   ☐ Psychiatrist   ☐ Pediatrician/Other Physician   ☐ Social Worker

☐ Counselor   ☐ Educator   ☐ Other (please describe) _____

☐ Please send me information about, *What to do When Your Child has Obsessive-Compulsive Disorder: Strategies and Solutions.*

Lighthouse Press, Inc.
www.Lighthouse-Press.com
Toll Free USA: 1-888-749-8768

MAIL YOUR COMPLETED ORDER FORM WITH YOUR CHECK/MONEY ORDER TO:
Lighthouse Press, Inc., 35 Ryans Run, Rochester, NY 14624

Lighthouse Press: ORDER FORM

NAME: _____

ADDRESS: _____

CITY: _____ STATE: _____ ZIP: _____ COUNTRY: _____

TELEPHONE: _____ E-MAIL ADDRESS: _____

Please send me _____ copies of *Up and Down the Worry Hill* by Aureen P. Wagner, Ph.D. for **$16.95** per book.

Quantity discount: If you are ordering at least 5 copies, deduct 15% from the total cost of the books.
Sales Tax: Please add applicable sales tax for those orders shipped to addresses in New York State.

SHIPPING AND HANDLING:

US: Add $3 shipping and handling for the first book and $1 for each additional book. **Canada:** Add $6 shipping and handling for the first book and $2 for each additional book. **Other International:** Please add $9 for the first book and $5 for each additional book.

ORDER TOTAL
$16.95 Per book x _____ books . . . . $_____
Quantity Discount (Subtract 15% if ordering 5 or more copies) – $_____
New York State Sales Tax . . . . $_____
Shipping and Handling (US/Canada/Int'l) . . . . $_____
TOTAL . . . . $_____

All orders must be prepaid by check/money order in US funds (checks drawn on US banks). Check enclosed for the amount of: $ _____

I am a/an:

☐ Parent ☐ Psychologist ☐ Psychiatrist ☐ Pediatrician/Other Physician ☐ Social Worker

☐ Counselor ☐ Educator ☐ Other (please describe) _____

☐ Please send me information about, *What to do When Your Child has Obsessive-Compulsive Disorder: Strategies and Solutions.*

Lighthouse Press, Inc.
www.Lighthouse-Press.com
Toll Free USA: 1-888-749-8768

MAIL YOUR COMPLETED ORDER FORM WITH YOUR CHECK/MONEY ORDER TO:
Lighthouse Press, Inc., 35 Ryans Run, Rochester, NY 14624